MY Forest school Journal

Dedicated to the children everywhere who are wild and free and eager to create and learn.

This Journal is perfect for recording all of the special things your children create in their early years and is perfect to keep a lasting memento of their wonderful activities and achievements.

Name

Date

Date	Activity

Date

Activity

Date

Activity

Date	Activity

Date	Activity

Date	Activity

Date

Activity

Date

Activity

Date	Activity

Date	Activity

Date	Activity

Date

Activity

Date

Activity

Date	Activity

Date	Activity

Date

Activity

Date

Activity

Date	Activity

Date	Activity

Date

Activity

Date

Activity

Date	Activity

Date	Activity

Date	Activity

Date

Activity

Date

Activity

Date

Activity

Date

Activity

Date	Activity

Date

Activity

Date	Activity

Date	Activity

Date

Activity

Date	Activity

Date

Activity

Date

Activity

Date	Activity

Date

Activity

Date	Activity

Date

Activity

Date

Activity

Date	Activity

Date	Activity

Date	Activity

Date

Activity

Date

Activity

Date

Activity

Date

Activity

Date	Activity

Date

Activity

Date

Activity

Date	Activity

Date	Activity

Date	Activity

Date

Activity

Date

Activity

Date

Activity

Date

Activity

Date	Activity

Date

Activity

Date

Activity

Date

Activity

Date	Activity

Date	Activity

Date

Activity

Date

Activity

Date	Activity

Date

Activity

Date	Activity

Date

Activity

Date

Activity

Date

Activity

Date	Activity

Notes:_____

_____

_____

_____

_____

_____

_____

_____

Notes:_____
_____
_____
_____
_____
_____
_____
_____

Notes:_____

_____

_____

_____

_____

_____

_____

_____

Notes:_____
_____
_____
_____
_____
_____
_____
_____

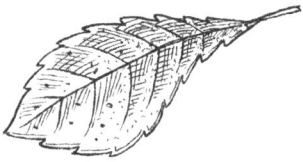

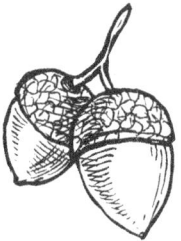

MADE

In the highlands

For more Journals visit our author
page:
www.amazon.com/author/
madejournals

Made in the USA
Las Vegas, NV
26 February 2022